Dear Lord
When You came into my life
With Your immeasurable love
And liberating power
Something wonderful happened.
Day after day
Year after year
It keeps happening . . .
And happening . . .
And happening. . . .

Lord, It Keeps Happening ...and Happening

RUTH HARMS CALKIN

LIVING BOOKS
Tyndale House Publishers, Inc.
Wheaton, Illinois

Third printing, October 1984
Library of Congress Catalog Card Number 83-91404
ISBN 0-8423-3823-3, paper
Copyright © 1984 by Ruth Harms Calkin
All rights reserved
Printed in the United States of America

CONTENTS

New Beginning

NEW BEGINNING

O God
What shall I do?
I am at the total end
Of myself.

Wonderful, dear child!
Now start your new beginning
With Me.

REJOICE!

O God
When I think of my selfishness
My hasty, unkind words
My bitterness
My shallowness and pride
My heart grieves.

My child, rejoice!
Your future is spotless.

CHRISTMAS DECLARATION

No one in our family
Has ever forgotten
Grandmother's favorite holiday declaration:
"Christmas!
A long time coming.
And so soon gone."
Year after year she said it with a sigh
As her tiny frame helped us gather
Torn boxes
Crumpled tissue
And tangled ribbons.
Even after Grandmother left us
Somebody in the family always remembered
And lovingly mimicked her:
"Christmas!
A long time coming
And so soon gone."

O Lord, thank You, thank You!
Though the historical event of Your birth
Was a long time coming
Never again need we wait for You.
Now and forever Your Presence is here.
With You there is no once-a-year Christmas.
Your gifts of mercy are new every morning
And fresh every evening.
And because You have promised
Never to leave us or forsake us
You are never "so soon gone."

AUTUMN GLOW

Lord, if You will make
The autumn of my life
As lovely as this
Golden autumn morning
I will not look back to grieve
The passing days of summer.
Of all the regal seasons
Autumn is most brilliant.
Make my life brilliant, too!

ON NEW YEAR'S DAY

O Lord God
Ye are able.

Able to make me clean
Without self-righteousness and sham.
Able to make me real
Without hypocrisy.

You are able
To give me wisdom
In all my priorities
My decisions, my goals.

You are able
To transform my fears
Into vibrant faith
And quiet trust.

You are able
To make this present year
The most challenging
The most productive
Of all my life.

On the first day of this new year
I covenant with You, dear God.
Please work in me
To the very depth of my being.

Renovate me
Transform me
For You are able—miraculously able
To make all things new.

HAPPY BIRTHDAY

Today is my birthday, Lord
And birthdays always excite me.
I am so like a little child
Breathlessly anticipating the surprises
Of a fresh, untarnished year.
As I reach out
Toward whatever moments or days
You entrust to me
Will there be drastic changes?
Will I be different?

My child
You are now
And always will be
Whatever you are willing
To let my love
Make of you.
Happy birthday!

TO THE NEW YEAR

Mysterious New Year
So wrapped in reserve and surprise
You have no reason to feel smug
Or even condescending.
After all, the majestic God
Has full knowledge of you
Just as He has of me.
There is not an issue that you can evade.
Furthermore, you are powerless
To do anything to me
That God does not permit.
All He allows in His infinite wisdom
Is for my ultimate good
And His greatest glory.
Consequently, New Year
You cannot trick or disillusion me
By your baffling unexplainables
Or your feverish activity.
My times are in the hands
Of my sovereign God
Whose power is limitless
And whose love for me is everlasting.

THE SECRET

I couldn't help but watch her
As we sat in the service together
Last Sunday morning . . .
Her white hair so neatly coiffured
Her hands resting on her open Bible
Her smile so beautifully tranquil.
When the hymn was announced
She sang with a glowing smile.
Occasionally during the message
She nodded her head in assent.
(O Lord, what peace she portrays.)
After the service I spoke to her:
"You are an inspiration, my dear.
I hope I may sit with you again."
She thanked me profusely.
Then she added with shining joy
"Isn't it wonderful to know Jesus?
I mean—really KNOW Him!"
In that instant, dear God
I knew the secret of her radiance.

ALL

O God
Thank You, thank You
For Your reiterated ALL...

You have promised:
    ALL my needs shall be supplied.
    ALL grace shall abound toward me.
    ALL the promises are mine.
    ALL things asked I shall receive.
    ALL sufficiency for ALL things.
    You are with me always
    ALL the days.
    And today!

PENITENT

O God
You have driven me into a corner
Where I cannot escape.
I come to You penitently
For today I've sinned grievously.
I have betrayed my highest ideals.
I have been false to my inner convictions.
I know I have broken Your heart.
Thank You for dealing with me
In the privacy of Your personal Presence
For my sin has been against You alone.
Cleanse me, Lord.
Change me.
Sin is so hideous, so outrageous!
Renew me until I am spiritually contagious.

FED UP

Lord, I'm utterly fed up
With my foolish and futile attempt
To live a facsimile of genuine Christianity.
Like thousands of jagged Christians
I am just so "sick and tired
Of being sick and tired."
I want to withdraw my membership
From the Society of Self-Improvement
With its heavy dues and dismal news.
With all my breathless effort
I am no further improved
Than the day I joined.
So please take me as I am
And make me what I could never be
Apart from You: transparently real!

RELEASE

You are showing me, Lord
That when I cling to negative thoughts
Regarding the actions of my family
I thwart Your divine purpose
And turn their actions upon myself.
I am beginning to grasp
That I must *release* to You
What I too often *resent* in others.

FACE TO FACE

O Lord God
Nothing in all of life
Brings as much glorious freedom
And total satisfaction
As the determination to stand with You
Against the insidious forces of evil—
To defy them in Your all-powerful Name.
It's like standing with Moses
At the top of the mountain
Meeting You face to face!

I STAKE MY LIFE

I stake my life totally
Completely
Permanently
On the integrity of Jesus.
Lord, Your integrity means
You will do all You promised.
You will see me through
Every fiery furnace
Every tempestuous storm.
If not, dear God
Then nothing in life
Makes any sense whatever.
Your part is to perform
What You promised.
My part is to trust and obey.

THE EXCEPTION

Lord, too often I demand
From my family and friends
More love
More affirmation
More acceptance
Than they are capable of giving.
Today, dear God
I ask You to burn this truth
Into the depth of my inner being:
Nobody in all the world
Can ever love me
As much as I need to be loved—
Except You!

GOD-GIVEN

Thank You, Lord
For one enchanted moment
To lift my eyes
Toward the veiled horizon
And give You praise
For another God-given day!

GOOD MORNING, LORD!

Good morning, Lord!
At the fresh, fragrant beginning
Of this new-born day
I give You my will
To blend with Yours.
I give You, in fact
My total self.
As I yield to Your instructions
I am joyfully confident
That You will take care of the obstructions.

UNNECESSARY

How patiently You wait, dear God
Until having battered myself
Against the impregnable wall
Of my own selfishness and rebellion
I turn at last
Broken and bruised
Into Your wide-open arms.
It is then that I learn
That all my struggling, my panic
My foolish pretenses were unnecessary—
Had I simply fallen trustingly
Into Your waiting arms
At the very beginning.

COMMONPLACE DAYS

Lord of my commonplace days
Forgive me for foolishly waiting
For "divine inspiration"
Before moving in on the tasks
Personally assigned to me.
Hopefully I am learning
To face with greater determination
The day-by-day drudgery
The trite, mundane tasks
The pushing-pulling glamourless duties.
Lord, even when I think
I'm getting no place
Keep me pushing on and on
With purpose and direction.
Grab my heart and quiet me
When I begin to whine and whimper.
Despite the daily drain
I think I see it more clearly now:
It is only when I begin to *do*
That You begin to *bless.*

TURNABOUT

God, for so long
I thought that by praying
I could change Your mind.
Often I prayed
Fervently, pleadingly
Until I felt
Emotionally pulverized.
Then I gradually began to grasp
That the purpose of prayer
Is to find *Your* mind
And let You change mine.
Little by little
The turnabout is renewing me.
Slowly I begin to feel
A settling quietness.
I wait while You woo me
To Your will, dear Lord.
I wait until my thoughts
Harmonize with Yours.
For in my deepest heart
Despite my guarded resistance
I somehow sense
That what You want for me
Is stupendously more
Than anything I could
Dream or wish or want
For myself.

HOW TO ENTERTAIN

Lord, I'm so glad
We don't have to be creative geniuses
Or serve elegant gourmet meals
To make our guests feel warm and wanted.
We need rather to expose them to love
And introduce them to laughter.
We need to listen
And never drown them out.
Above all, we need to remember
That there is no substitute—
None whatever—
For concentrated sharing
And genuine caring.

I BEGIN TO WONDER

Sometimes, dear God
As I read Your Word
It so pierces my heart
And analyzes my emotions
That I am left bare
And defenseless before You.
Then I begin to wonder
If the Bible *starts* with Revelation
And *ends* with Revolution!

WHAT DO YOU SAY TO THAT?

His divorce had just become final.
He was seething with bitterness.
"Women! Stupid women"
He said angrily.
"They've been no good
From the very beginning.
Remember? It was a woman—
A woman named Eve
Who brought deceit into the world.
What do you say to that?"

"But sir, have you forgotten?
It was a woman—
A woman named Mary
Who brought the Savior into the world.
Sir, what do you say to that?"

It Keeps
Happening

IT KEEPS HAPPENING

Dear Lord
When You came into my life
With Your immeasurable love
And liberating power
Something wonderful happened.
Day after day
Year after year
It keeps happening . . .
And happening . . .
And happening . . . .

SURE GUARANTEE

Early this morning, Lord
As we read Your Word aloud
You captured our attention
With the psalmist's declaration
"Oh, magnify the Lord with me
And let us exalt his name together."
My husband said thoughtfully
"If we'll do it day by day—
If we'll really exalt His name *together*
We'll have a sure guarantee
For a *forever* marriage."
The thought became a melody
Singing in my heart all day.
Lord, that's why I felt compelled
To write today's date
And the words *forever together*
In the margin next to the verse.
Now help us to do it!

I PRAISE YOU

I praise You, my Lord!
I praise You for all things:
For this very moment
For future days
For the past
Often so reckless
On my part
So filled with
Foolish fantasies.
But so gracious
On Your part
So loving
And so totally forgiving.
I praise You!

SAD FACSIMILE

Lord, I am ashamed!
Too often I have asked You
To do whatever You wish with me.
But I am never quite content
Unless You wish to make of me
Something flattering
Something spectacular
Something colorful and praiseworthy
For all the world to see.
What a sad facsimile
Of genuine spirituality.

YOU ALONE

Lord
Make me a woman
After Your own heart.
I want this so much.
For YOU, dear Lord, I want this.
Transform me, liberate me
From my fumbling, my stumbling
My glaring weaknesses.
God, I don't want to hide
Behind a smiling mask.
I want to reflect the image
Of the Son of God.
You alone can make it happen!

THE CHOICE

Lord, it never fails.
Every time I speak to women
About total commitment
You always whisper
"Prove it!"
And I see that I have
One choice and an alternate:
I stop speaking
Or I prove it.

SLOW GROWTH

In my fretful impatience
I am so often inclined to ask
"Why can't she change?"
"Why is he always so slow?"
"Will they ever learn from past mistakes?"
And then You begin to impress me
With my own slow progress upward.
I see Your stretched-out patience.
I remember how long You've waited for me.
And I grieve that my attitude
Is so often intolerant.
O God, keep fresh the imprint
Of my own need to grow
And make me more flexible
More understanding
And always more loving.

THE CHALLENGE

I remember so vividly
The challenge of theological discussions
During long-ago college years.
Even today I enjoy the stimulation
Of a rousing debate
Concerning biblical concepts.
But, Lord, as I listen
Or become defensive
Or attempt to communicate
Please don't ever let me forfeit a promise
By clinging stubbornly to a prejudice.

PURE AND SIMPLE

God, so often I have heard You say
"Obedience—that's the thing with Me."
Just pure and simple obedience
Is what You ask.
In big things
Little things
Ordinary things.
The joy comes after obeying.
Or perhaps more accurately
The joy comes *in* obeying.
I have no excuse.
You assure me I can do
Everything You ask me to do
By Your continual enabling power.
I know, too
That nothing in the world
Gives greater peace
Or greater security
Than faithful obedience—
Day by day, hour after hour.
And yet, dear God
I achingly confess
I am prone to ignore Your commands.
Deliberately I disregard Your nudges.
Lord, may it be different today—
Much different!
Today may I obey all the way!

I SHOUT FOR JOY

Sometimes, Lord
You seem a million miles away
And then I remember Your unfailing words:
"I will never, never let go of your hand."
Once again I shout for joy
That what *seems* to be
Is not always what *is*.

HIS NAME

Looking down at her coffee cup
She asked casually
"What do you believe about God?"
We began a discussion
Of conflicting ideas and concepts
With no positive conclusions whatever.
"Whom do you trust?" I finally asked
And immediately the Name *Jesus*
United our searching hearts.

ENTANGLED

"I want to be unentangled"
She told me years ago.
"I hate taking orders
From God or anyone else."
All the rest of her life
She became so entangled
With her own miserable self
That she lived in deep depression
Until the day she died.

O God
I want to be forever
Entangled with You!

IN THE END

God, it is not always easy
To know and do Your will.
But of this I am wholly convinced:
In the end, nothing else matters.

THE REASON

O God
Why am I so distraught
So fearfully overwatchful?

Disturbed child
It is because
You no longer cast your care
On the One who watches you.

WHAT WOULD HAPPEN?

Lord, thank You for the dear woman
Who long ago said to my preacher-father
"Every morning at six o'clock
I fervently pray for you."

God, I wonder . . .
What would happen in churches
Across our land
If every morning at six o'clock
A dozen faithful members
In every church
Prayed fervently for their pastor.

The You
Means
Me

THE YOU MEANS ME

O my Father, my Father!
At this crisis time of my life
When I feel trampled and battered
I know it is imperative
For me to remember
That the nature of my problem
Is not the significant thing.
The significant thing
Is the nature of You
My refuge. My rock.
My high tower.
There is no situation
Anytime, or anywhere
Of which I cannot confidently say
"For this I have Him."
But I am so quick to forget
And so prone to neglect.
Lord, may I get it settled
Once and for all
That when You say
"My peace I give unto you"
The *you* means *me!*

ANTIQUES

Today I spent two happy hours
With a beautiful young woman
Who loves antiques.
In every room of her charming home
There is superb evidence of her ability
To choose the genuine.
As we sat at her round oak table
Drinking a cup of cinnamon-spiced tea
I laughed aloud
At her spontaneous remark:
"Sometimes I wonder
If God minds living here.
After all, He makes all things new."

Lord, thank You for the reminder
Of Your magnificent promise:
"Behold, I make all things new."
And thank You for the shining creativity
You've entrusted to a dedicated young woman
Who loves You far more than antiques.

SUDDENLY OR FINALLY

Right now, dear God
In my bewildering day of turmoil
I call upon You
With unashamed boldness.
I come to You directly
Before seeking out family or friends.
You have promised to extricate me
According to Your infallible Word.
I offer You now my sacrifice of praise
For I know my deliverance will come.
"He is faithful that promised."
And, dear Lord, when You do deliver me
Whether it be suddenly or finally
I pledge my continual gratitude.
In fact, You'll never hear the end of it!

ALWAYS THINKING

Thinking, always thinking. . . .

Again today, dear Lord
I think of my friend
And the miserable quarrel
That shattered our friendship
After years of beautiful closeness. . . .

I think of the soloist
I refuse to acknowledge
On a worshipful Sunday morning
Because of envy and pride. . . .

I think of the young mother
Down the street
Deserted and divorced
Picking up bits and pieces. . . .

The wrinkled old woman
Languishing in a rest home
Who for many faithful years
Taught me from God's Word. . . .

Thinking, always thinking. . . .

Lord, if suddenly You said
"This is your last week
On the planet called Earth"
How quickly, how spontaneously
My thoughts would convert to action.

How eagerly I would do
In seven short days
What You've persistently pressed upon me
For the past several months.
Lord, is it too late?

"And they immediately . . . followed him"
   (Matthew 4:20).

YOU SHOW YOURSELF STRONG

Dear Lord, Your Word says
Your eyes search back and forth
Across the whole earth
To show Yourself strong
On behalf of those
Whose hearts are in harmony with Yours.
As You search back and forth
At six o'clock each morning, dear God,
I know You see me
As I reluctantly crawl
From under the soft blankets
And stumble in the dark
Toward my living room trysting place.
It isn't easy to cater
To the clanging alarm
Especially on cold winter mornings
When my will is so weak
And the bed feels so warm.
But after an hour of meditation and prayer
You miraculously renew me
And my spirit is wonderfully restored.
Thank You for showing Yourself strong
On my behalf, dear Lord
As I sit in my brown chair
Reading Your Word and
Hearing Your voice
At six o'clock in the morning.

PAINFULLY NEW

O God
This sudden catastrophe
Is tearing my heart.
How can I endure it?
Why are You permitting it?
I know I am not alone.
All over the world
Your children are asking Why.
It's an old, old question—
As old as Job.
But today for me
It is painfully new.

I WILL WAIT

O Lord
Today I must face it honestly with You
By pursuing the persistent questions within me:

God, is there any gain at all by my doubting?
Do doubts make me stronger?
Do they purify my heart? Fortify my will?
Are my emotions firmly established by my
    doubts?
Are my family and friends encouraged?

On the other hand, God
Even though I see no possible way out
Of the catastrophe I now face
Is there anything more pleasing to You
Than my personal choice to trust You?
I know it is true, Lord
I must rely on Your promises in the end.
Would You be glorified, dear God
If I trusted You now at the early beginning?

O God, forgive me
For so limiting You.
Surely You know exactly what You will do.
You are God, so You will not alter Your Word.
Your power is instantly operative
In all the strange twisting of my life.
You are God, so You are good.

I will hope
I will trust
I will wait
On the living God!

INTIMATE CLOSENESS

You promise, dear God
That when I draw close to You
You will draw close to me.
Lord, I give myself to You unreservedly.
Teach me more and more
Of intimate closeness
And fill my heart with You alone.
To walk arm-in-arm with You
Down every winding path
Seems to me
The dearest of all delights.

THE HARDEST THING

O God
In these crisis days
Of piercing pain
And emotional fatigue
Do a brand new thing in me.
Give me water in the wilderness
And streams in my desert.
You have promised to be my God
Through all my lifetime.
Surely You will keep Your word!

As You promised
Give me rest from my sorrow
And from my fear
And from the bondage
That binds me.
One thing more, dear Lord:
Enable me to praise You
When to praise
Is the hardest thing of all.

DIFFICULT

Lord
Sometimes
I find it
Intolerably difficult
To tell You
The exact truth
About myself.

I TRUST

O God, thank You
That Your promises are valid
As long as the world lasts.
They do not suddenly dissolve
When my faith is feeble
And my courage fails.
When You have given a promise
You will perform it—
Sight or no sight
Feeling or no feeling.

You may take me
Through the darkest night
The deepest waters.
The very worst may happen
But out of it
You will bring the very best
For Your Word remains secure.

Lord, keep me faithful in my trust.
When I can articulate no other prayer
May my waiting heart
Continually avow:
I trust!
I trust!

HELP ME TO LISTEN

Dear Lord
Help me to *listen* to my husband
Without misinterpreting—
Without interrupting.
Don't let me color his words
With my own preconceived ideas.
Keep me from barging in
With "that reminds me . . ."
And, Lord, may I never use ridicule
As a symbol of superiority.

REAL REASON

Lord, whenever I must cringe
Because of spiritual defeat
I know it is because
I have an Adversary.

Child of my protecting care
Whenever you must cringe
Because of spiritual defeat
It is because
You give in to the Adversary.

ENOUGH GRACE

Lord of my trembling heart . . .
If there is enough ocean
To keep one small fish swimming
Then surely there is enough grace
To keep one weak child standing.

I SING IN THE RAIN

One cold, misty day
When I was nine years old
I walked hand-in-hand
Through a wooded forest
With my strong, gentle father.
"Listen to the stillness," he whispered.
"Stillness makes beautiful music."
Suddenly he pointed to a tiny bird
Perched on a limb of a bending tree.
"The bird doesn't know we're here
But he's singing his heart out."
Then smiling down at me he asked
"Could you sing in the rain
If nobody heard you but God?"

Lord, though many years have passed
Since I walked with my father
I have never forgotten his question.
Today I am alone—
Yet not alone, for YOU are here.
Though my heart is grief-drenched
I know You are worthy of praise.
Help me, please help me
To sing my feeble song in the rain
Though nobody hears but You.

LISTEN TRUSTINGLY

Lord, I'm listening.
Why don't I hear You?

Fretful child
You listen
Strenuously
Anxiously
Laboriously.

Rest in Me
And listen
Trustingly.
I am talking
All the time.

SANE ESTIMATE

Lord, help me to face with honesty
And genuine appreciation
The talents and abilities
You have given
As special gifts to me.
Give me a sane estimate of myself.
Neither exaggerated nor mud-crawling.
Just *sane,* as Your Word admonishes.
May I be joyfully satisfied
With Your unique plan for me.
When at times I'd secretly love to ride
On a colorful float
Beautifully adorned
Waving to cheering crowds
Smile at me, Lord.
With a twinkle in Your eye
Remind me again
That somebody has to build the float.

ONLY A FEELING

Lord
I don't like feeling
Like a half-person.

My child
It is only a feeling.
You are complete in Me.

INSUPERABLY DIFFICULT

Lord, I am discovering
How insuperably difficult it is
To give what You ask of me.
You never take less than all.

DISCIPLINED ONE

Today I promised myself
I wouldn't eat a bite of candy—
Not a single bite.
I kept that promise.
I promised myself
I'd walk two miles
And I walked almost three.
I kept that promise.
I promised myself
I'd clean the messy refrigerator.
I kept that promise.
I promised myself
I'd read a magazine article
About choosing priorities.
I kept that promise.
I promised myself
There would be no bedtime snack.
I cheated. I failed.
I just couldn't resist
Those crackers with the tangy cheese.
(At least I *didn't* resist.)
Well, four out of five promises kept—
That's at least better than yesterday.

O Lord
I struggle so with discipline!
Sometimes the very word depresses me.
Nevertheless, keep turning me
Toward the right direction.

Even though a detour from time to time
Doesn't mean total defeat
I do so long for the rugged strength
That discipline always builds.
Forcefully remind me, dear God
That unbridled behavior
Always leads to discontent.
I really want to follow You, Lord
And a disciple is a disciplined one!

Moment
Memories

LORD OF LITTLE BOYS

She was standing at the kitchen sink
Peeling potatoes for dinner
When suddenly Casey burst in.
Casey—young and eager
All boy, a giant joy.
He wanted to know
"Will you tell me a story?"
"A story? You mean NOW?"
"Sure, Mom.
The one about Gramps
Getting locked in the church."
"Well, I'll have to keep working
While I tell it.
It's almost dinnertime."
"That's OK. I'll follow you around."

Lord of little boys . . .
He is so full of
Zest and energy
Mischief and adventure
Stumbling and tumbling
Running and reaching
Yawning and stretching
I'm surprised he has time
To listen at all!

Thank You for interludes
In the midst of busy days—

Interludes that build
Priceless memories
For very special mothers
And very special boys.

MEMORIES

Dear God
How I thank You
For thousands of beautiful memories
That have become a growing history
Of Your supreme goodness in my life.
Thank You for misty memories
Flaming memories, trailing memories.
Thank You for throbbing memories
Quiet, gentle memories
Pink-tinted memories
That live on and on
To gladden somber days.
Thank You for memories that have rooted me
Stabilized me, sensitized me
And toughened the inner fiber of my being.
In Your honor, dear God
I erect my *Monument of Memories.*
For Your glory . . . You who are
My "living bright Reality."

EXPLANATION

Just this week
I read a newspaper account
Of a thirteen-year-old boy
Who saved his brother's life
By driving him to a hospital
In his father's car.
Never having driven before
His explanation was simple:
"I just did what I saw my father do."

O dear God
Please empower me to bring life
To a sick, wounded world
With the simple explanation:
"I do what my Father does."

MY HUSBAND AT WORK

Lord
As my husband goes to his office today
I send him off with a hug and a prayer.
Thank You for the security I feel
In knowing You'll be with him all the way.
Protect him, dear God
As he maneuvers through heavy traffic.
Keep him relaxed as he changes lanes
And waits for signal lights.
Fill him with anticipation
Despite the annoyance he often feels
As he grapples with office personnel.
Should irritating problems remain unsolved
Please, Lord, lift him above them.
Make him resolute against discouragement.
May he *trust* Your guidance
Even though he may not *feel* it.
Whatever his achievements
Whatever his defeats
Bring him home at the end of the day
With the quiet assurance
That Your promises are positive
Your power exceeds all pressure
And our home is his fortress.

THE GIFT

I heard today
Of a decrepit native woman
Who walked mile after mile
Under the blistering sun
To bring a small gift of embroidery
To the missionary she deeply loved.
Hour after hour she trudged
Over rough, rugged roads
Clutching tightly her small gift.
Her weary body sagged
Her vision blurred
Her bare feet bled from the jagged rocks.

Grateful but overwhelmed
The missionary wept.
The trembling old woman spoke softly:
"Please understand.
The walk is part of the gift."

My Lord
My commitment to You is for life.
I give myself to You unreservedly
To do with me as You please.
But may I not forget
That the tears, the fears
The strain and the pain
The sunless days
The starless nights
Are all a part of the whole.

In my total commitment
I give full consent:
The walk is part of the gift.

HOW, LORD?

Lord
Here I am at a mountain retreat
Surrounded by 300 women
Who are apparently delighted to be here.
But with all my heart
I wish I hadn't come.
I feel totally inadequate
And very, very lonely.
It isn't that the women are unfriendly
It's just that I'm so fearful
Of making myself vulnerable.
Lord, I just don't like group discussions
Where we talk about personal needs!
Sometimes I say things so stupidly
Or I stutter over simple words
Or I worry about being accepted.

Something else, Lord:
I'm not sure I brought the right clothes.
And of all times for my hair
To be flying in every direction!
I'm sure I'm trying too hard
And smiling too much
In an effort to put myself over
But the fear of rejection overwhelms me.
Lord, when I registered for the retreat
The thought of a weekend
Free from dishes and dusting delighted me

But right now I'd love to be washing dishes
In the security of my own small kitchen.

I wonder—
Was it wrong for me to come
Or am I simply refusing Your invitation
To step out of my wretched self
Into the "glorious freedom
Of the children of God"?
O Lord, why do I even ask?
Deep in my heart I know.
But how do I do it, Lord?
How?

MORBID MEMORIES

Lord, I can't mow down morbid memories
Like my husband mows tall grass.
Mercilessly they take revenge
By tramping gleefully
Through my somber heart.
So, dear Lord
I ask YOU to shake them
In the sunlight of Your love.
Then may the gentle breeze
Of the Holy Spirit
Blow them all away—
Never to be found again.

SO SPIRITUAL

Why is it, Lord
That I can be "so spiritual"
At a Bible study or a retreat?
Beautiful thoughts form!
Inspiring words flow!
But in the midst of frustration
Or disappointment
Or weariness or stress
The contrast is sadly astounding.
God, I feel deeply convicted.
I see that I am too often
"Enchanted but unchanged."

NOW

My great, strong God!
All the fight
Is drained out of me.
In my debilitating weakness
I can't even hold on to You.
But Your own words
Keep my hope stirring:
"For I your God
Am firmly grasping
Your right hand.
I am saying unto you
Do not fear.
I have become your helper."
Now, dear Lord!
Now!

SOUNDPROOF

God of penitent hearts
The moment Your prophet Isaiah
Knew You had cleansed his sin
At that very moment
He heard Your Voice
Addressed directly to him.
Lord, thank You
For the revealing discovery
That only one thing
Makes me soundproof
Against Your Voice:
My refusal to relinquish my sin.

SPIRITUAL MATHEMATICS

Lord
Today I suddenly remember
Something my father said years ago
As we sat at our dinner table
When we were children:
"If I have a dollar
And you have a dollar
And we exchange those dollars
We still each have one dollar.
But if I have a thought
And you have a thought
And we exchange those thoughts
We each have two thoughts."

Several hours from now, Lord
I'll be eating lunch
With a group of very special women.
We'll be expressing ideas
Sharing concepts
Exchanging thoughts.
O God, give us, I pray
The mind of Christ.
May His expressed thoughts through us
Multiply a thousand times
And leave indelible impressions
Of Your magnificent love.

LONG-AGO MEMORIES

Tonight, long-ago memories
Have been wandering down
Old familiar streets
And dark alleys
And dimly lit corridors.
With stubborn tenacity
They invade my carefully guarded defenses.
Sitting all alone watching dreams go by
I discover unexpectedly
That I am still susceptible to tears.
And then I recall vaguely
Part of an old song that says
"For these tears I died"
And my yearning heart, dear Lord
Reaches out for You.

My
Personal
Rainbow

MY PERSONAL RAINBOW

Lord, right now
I struggle with clutching fear.
Waves of agony pour over me
As I face the darkest moments
In my life's history.
But my conviction still stands firm:
You are my God!
And though I cannot predict my future
Or even tomorrow
I am sustained by the reminder
That the longest storm
The world has ever known . . .
And the worst . . .
Came to an end one clear-sky morning.
It was true for Noah
It will be true for me.
Though as yet I see no deliverance
I watch
I wait
I expect
My personal rainbow.

PERFECT TIMING

O God
How perfect is Your timing!
You always seem to send
The right person at the right time.
Or a song that comforts.
Or a note that encourages.
Or somebody brings a pie
And it doesn't matter at all
That I'm not a bit hungry—
The pie spells love
And love satisfies my heart-hunger.
You fill the air with surprises
And the night with stars
And when at moments
There is the painful temptation
To give in to despair
You break through the darkness
With Your comforting words
"I'm right here."

SURGE OF LONGING

O dear God
Deep within me
There is a great surge of longing
To say thank you
To Amy Carmichael
For her words that come
Like refreshing rain
To my parched heart:
"Until this tyranny be overpast
Thy hand will hold me fast."
Lord, please thank her for me!

RELATIONSHIP

Lord
As You show me
That You are my Father
By instructing me
May I show You
That I am Your child
By obeying You.

THE MINISTRY OF LETTERS

Lord, sometimes I think
I can't strike another typewriter key.
I can't write another paragraph or word.
I can't even put a period
At the end of a sentence.
I look at the fat bundle
Of unanswered letters
And it all seems so futile
So time-consuming, so unending.
I can't think or concentrate.
What I write seems empty, lifeless.
I struggle to keep my thoughts coherent.
Yet, I know I must keep on.
I have committed myself
To a ministry of writing—
Writing letters!

And often, God, when I begin to question
My personal commitment
You send me a ray of hope . . .
A personal rainbow.
Someone stops me to say
"Ten years ago, when I needed it most
You sent me a letter of encouragement.
I've read it a hundred times.
It's worn and tear-stained
But I'll treasure it forever."

Lord, I don't even remember writing.
It's been so long.
But it doesn't matter.
I see again the value of ministry
And so I'll continue.
But first, Lord
I must put a period after the sentence
I so wearily wrote just an hour ago.

BURNING BUSHES

O God
I come to You penitently just now
Confessing I have spent
Far too many hours
Exploring the dramatic
The ecstatic, the sensational.
I have been much too engrossed
In looking for burning bushes.
All the while
You have been waiting for me
To take off my shoes
Bow before You
And crown You LORD of my life.

THE GREAT CONTRAST

"He is not here."
Unparalleled sadness!

"He is risen
As He said."
Unquenchable gladness!

YOUR WORD

Your Word!
O God, how it pierces
The deepest recesses of my being.
It analyzes every secret emotion
And leaves me exposed and defenseless.
At times Your Word is like fire
Burning up my pettiness, my petulance.
Or like a steady hammer
Shattering to dust my tolerated conflicts.
At other times it is like a gentle voice
Spreading great calm over my restless mind.
O Lord, I can never be content
To dabble in a chapter here and there
Or skim a verse or two
For always You confront me personally
And I know that I am looking
Beyond earth and sky
Into the very face of God.

BALANCED FRIENDSHIP

My Father, my Friend!
I long for us to have
The kind of balanced friendship
That existed between You and Abraham.
You gave Abraham all You promised
And Abraham gave You all the glory.

THE ONE FIXED POLE

Dear Lord, forgive me
For my foolish, desperate attempt
To win Heaven's blue ribbon
For the management
Of my own small world—
When deep in my bewildered heart
I know, *I do know*
That the one fixed pole
In all my hectic confusion
Is the faithfulness
Of the living God.

I DON'T UNDERSTAND

Lord
I just don't understand
What in the world
You're doing in my life.

My child
Don't try to understand.
Just live it
For Me.

NOT SURE YET

In our challenging discussion
I started to tell my college friend
That though I didn't understand electricity
I certainly accepted it.
With an impatient gesture he interrupted me.
"I don't want to hear about electricity.
I just want God."
"How much do you want Him?" I asked.
Nervous silence. Then finally a reply:
"I'm really not sure yet."

Lord, I don't know how long
My seeker-for-God friend
Will continue his flimsy excuses
Or linger in a state of noncommitment
But when he is sure enough to really seek You
He will surely find You.
This is Your personal promise.

SURPRISES

Ever since I was a little girl
I've loved surprises.
Frequently my mother would say
(Her eyes twinkling)
"I've got a surprise for you!"
I'd squeal with delight
And breathlessly wait.
The surprises were never elaborate—
Often just little trinkets—
But it was the very word *surprise*
That created the ecstasy.

I'm a grown woman now
(At least chronologically)
But there is still a little girl in me
Who loves surprises.
Lord, how I thank You
For knowing me so well.
You continually surprise me with joy!

FREEDOM

For so long, dear God
I stared with dreadful fascination
At the thick, heavy chains
Binding my burdened life
When all the while You were waiting
For my personal consent
To break the chains and set me free.
Oh, what liberating joy
When I finally said Yes!

THE SONG I SING

O dear God
Make me a woman of concern
And deep, deep compassion.
There is so much loneliness
So much despair and neglect
So much pain and disappointment
In the world today.
I see it all around me, Lord.
In my block, my church
In the homes of families and friends.
Make me achingly aware.
Let me care, let me share.
Lord, may I be at least one chord
Of beautiful music
In the heart of a mother
Or a father or a precious child
Where the longing for harmony
Lies so deeply hidden.
Above all, my Lord
Channel through me
Your matchless love
For You are the Song I joyfully sing.

YOUR FRIEND, TOO

Thank You, dear God
For my cherished friend
Who is Your friend, too.
Thank You for the vital contribution
She has made to my life
Through many shining years.
I have watched her spiritual growth
With awe and great excitement.
There have been painful places for her.
There have been hollow moments
And tear-soaked pillows.
But never did she give up.
She continued to pray big prayers
And claim big promises.
When she reached out toward You
She always discovered
Your hand was waiting for hers.
You took the doubt, the confusion
And rebuilt her faith.
You renewed her enthusiasm
Until she determined to make it
No matter what.
Thank You for that!

Lord, may she continue to sense
That I pray for her often.
I wish so many things for her:
Mountains to climb
And goals to pursue.

May she have freedom from anxiety
But never from accomplishment.
Above all, dear God
I pray for deep-down contentment
In her lifelong commitment to You.
Remind her often that her life
Is a fresh thought from You to the world.
May she always be able to say
With the sweet-singing psalmist
"He is the source of all my joy."

THE PAIN OF GROWTH

O God
Growth is a painful process.
I frankly confess
I am a coward about pain.
I don't like it, Lord.
I never pray for it
Or get excited over it.
In fact, I often resist it:
The pain of emotional trauma
So overwhelming
So baffling and crushing.
The deep-cutting pain
Of a broken relationship.
Physical pain that goes on and on
Until my entire body screams.
The pain of cruel cutting words.
The pain of loneliness, rejection
Or financial ruin.
The pain of being misunderstood.
Lord, the very thought of pain
Frightens and unnerves me.
Yet it is true—
Again and again it is true:
My greatest spiritual growth
Has come through pain.
Through heartache
And anguish.
And very often in my suffering
When I sadly thought

You were doing absolutely nothing
At that very moment
You were doing more *within* me
Than I ever dreamed or hoped.

SO DEMANDING

God, Your Word is so demanding.
It demands great stretches of my time—
Not just occasionally
But day after day, year after year.
I can't just grab a bite of it
With one hand in the dishwater
Or on the steering wheel
While I'm backing out of the garage.
Your Word insists that I ponder
That I contemplate and meditate
That I seriously apply it to my life.
It insists on obedience and forgiveness
On gentleness and love.
Its claim upon me is absolute.
Only as I obey
Can I know the peace
That passes all understanding.

But God
Its very insistence transforms me
For it proclaims Your faithfulness
In superlative terms.
As I give it my fixed, steady attention
My composure increases
My anxiety decreases
And I am supported on every side.
Jeremiah said, " . . . your word was unto me
The joy and rejoicing of my heart."

And in the margin of my Bible
Next to the words of the prophet
There is my own personal notation:
"My heart, too!"

BIRTHDAY PRAYER

"Make a wish! Make a wish!"
My gleeful family shouted
As I blew out the candles on my cake.
Lord, for this new year of my life
My "wish" becomes my personal prayer. . . .

I commit myself radically to You
With determined refusal
To settle for mediocrity.
As I courageously explore new vistas
And accept fresh challenges
Keep me on the growing edge.
Lord, if life becomes more difficult
Perhaps even more dangerous
Make it likewise increasingly productive.
I long to live life fully
With intensity and immensity.
At the same time make me flexible
Free from the turbulence so often created
By my own self-will.

O God, make me intuitively aware
Of those in serious need.
May I see grief through Your eyes
And do something about it.
May I reach out with Your sheltering arms
To touch, to care, to give.
I'm weary of *talking* love, Lord.

Talk can be so pious, so empty.
Teach me to practice loving
Until doors open and walls crumble
And wrongs are made right.
Until the great old hymn is true
In hearts and homes everywhere:
"When nothing else could help
Love lifted me."
Lord of all my moments
My days, my years
This is my birthday prayer.

THERE ARE NO WORDS

How can I put into words, my Lord
The flooding, transforming power
That sweeps my life because of You?
How can I explain to anyone
The soaring, surging peace
That You alone can give?
All the wonder-filled things in my life
All the joyful, glorious things
I owe to Your goodness
Your faithfulness
Your love.
Nothing is ever the same, my Lord
Since the day I met You.
And the longer I know You
The deeper my love.

Other Living Books Bestsellers

THE BEST CHRISTMAS PAGEANT EVER by Barbara Robinson. A delightfully wild and funny story about what can happen to a Christmas program when the "horrible Herdman" family of brothers and sisters are miscast in the roles of the Christmas story characters from the Bible. 07-0137 $2.50.

ELIJAH by William H. Stephens. He was a rough-hewn farmer who strolled onto the stage of history to deliver warnings to Ahab the king and to defy Jezebel the queen. A powerful biblical novel you will never forget. 07-4023 $3.50.

THE TOTAL MAN by Dan Benson. A practical guide on how to gain confidence and fulfillment. Covering areas such as budgeting of time, money matters, and marital relationships. 07-7289 $3.50.

HOW TO HAVE ALL THE TIME YOU NEED EVERY DAY by Pat King. Drawing from her own and other women's experiences as well as from the Bible and the research of time experts, Pat has written a warm and personal book for every Christian woman. 07–1529 $2.95.

IT'S INCREDIBLE by Ann Kiemel. "It's incredible" is what some people say when a slim young woman says, "Hi, I'm Ann," and starts talking about love and good and beauty. As Ann tells about a Jesus who can make all the difference in their lives, some call that incredible, and turn away. Others become miracles themselves, agreeing with Ann that it's incredible. 07–1818 $2.50.

EVERGREEN CASTLES by Laurie Clifford. A heartwarming story about the growing pains of five children whose hilarious adventures teach them unforgettable lessons about love and forgiveness, life and death. Delightful reading for all ages. 07-0779 $3.50.

JOHN, SON OF THUNDER by Ellen Gunderson Traylor. Travel with John down the desert paths, through the courts of the Holy City, and to the foot of the cross. Journey with him from his luxury as a privileged son of Israel to the bitter hardship of his exile on Patmos. This is a saga of adventure, romance, and discovery — of a man bigger than life — the disciple "whom Jesus loved." 07–1903 $3.95.

WHAT'S IN A NAME? compiled by Linda Francis, John Hartzel, and Al Palmquist. A fascinating name dictionary that features the literal meaning of people's first names, the character quality implied by the name, and an applicable Scripture verse for each name listed. Ideal for expectant parents! 07-7935 $2.95.

Other Living Books Bestsellers

THE MAN WHO COULD DO NO WRONG by Charles E. Blair with John and Elizabeth Sherrill. He built one of the largest churches in America . . . then he made a mistake. This is the incredible story of Pastor Charles E. Blair, accused of massive fraud. A book "for error-prone people in search of the Christian's secret for handling mistakes." 07–4002 $3.50.

GIVERS, TAKERS AND OTHER KINDS OF LOVERS by Josh McDowell. This book bypasses vague generalities about love and sex and gets right down to basic questions: Whatever happened to sexual freedom? What's true love like? What is your most important sex organ? Do men respond differently than women? If you're looking for straight answers about God's plan for love and sexuality then this book was written for you. 07–1031 $2.50.

MORE THAN A CARPENTER by Josh McDowell. This best selling author thought Christians must be "out of their minds." He put them down. He argued against their faith. But eventually he saw that his arguments wouldn't stand up. In this book, Josh focuses upon the person who changed his life — Jesus Christ. 07–4552 $2.50.

HIND'S FEET ON HIGH PLACES by Hannah Hurnard. A classic allegory which has sold more than a million copies! 07–1429 $3.50.

THE CATCH ME KILLER by Bob Erler with John Souter. Golden gloves, black belt, green beret, silver badge. Supercop Bob Erler had earned the colors of manhood. Now can he survive prison life? An incredible true story of forgiveness and hope. 07–0214 $3.50.

WHAT WIVES WISH THEIR HUSBANDS KNEW ABOUT WOMEN by Dr. James Dobson. By the best selling author of *DARE TO DISCIPLINE* and *THE STRONG-WILLED CHILD*, here's a vital book that speaks to the unique emotional needs and aspirations of today's woman. An immensely practical, interesting guide. 07–7896 $2.95.

PONTIUS PILATE by Dr. Paul Maier. This fascinating novel is about one of the most famous Romans in history — the man who declared Jesus innocent but who nevertheless sent him to the cross. This powerful biblical novel gives you a unique insight into the life and death of Jesus. 07–4852 $3.95.

BROTHER OF THE BRIDE by Donita Dyer. This exciting sequel to *THE BRIDE'S ESCAPE* tells of the faith of a proud, intelligent Armenian family whose Christian heritage stretched back for centuries. A story of suffering, separation, valor, victory, and reunion. 07–0179 $2.95.

LIFE IS TREMENDOUS by Charlie Jones. Believing that enthusiasm makes the difference, Jones shows how anyone can be happy, involved, relevant, productive, healthy, and secure in the midst of a high-pressure, commercialized, automated society. 07–2184 $2.50.

HOW TO BE HAPPY THOUGH MARRIED by Dr. Tim LaHaye. One of America's most successful marriage counselors gives practical, proven advice for marital happiness. 07–1499 $2.95.

Other Living Books Bestsellers

DAVID AND BATHSHEBA by Roberta Kells Dorr. Was Bathsheba an innocent country girl or a scheming adulteress? What was King David really like? Solomon — the wisest man in the world — was to be king, but could he survive his brothers' intrigues? Here is an epic love story which comes radiantly alive through the art of a fine storyteller. 07–0618 $3.95.

TOO MEAN TO DIE by Nick Pirovolos with William Proctor. In this action-packed story, Nick the Greek tells how he grew from a scrappy immigrant boy to a fearless underworld criminal. Finally caught, he was imprisoned. But something remarkable happened and he was set free — truly set free! 07–7283 $3.50.

FOR WOMEN ONLY. This bestseller gives a balanced, entertaining, diversified treatment of all aspects of womanhood. Edited by Evelyn and J. Allan Petersen, founder of Family Concern. 07–0897 $3.50.

FOR MEN ONLY. Edited by J. Allan Petersen, this book gives solid advice on how men can cope with the tremendous pressures they face every day as fathers, husbands, workers. 07–0892 $3.50.

ROCK. What is rock music really doing to you? Bob Larson presents a well-researched and penetrating look at today's rock music and rock performers. What are lyrics really saying? Who are the top performers and what are their life-styles? 07–5686 $2.95.

THE ALCOHOL TRAP by Fred Foster. A successful film executive was about to lose everything — his family's vacation home, his house in New Jersey, his reputation in the film industry, his wife. This is an emotion-packed story of hope and encouragement, offering valuable insights into the troubled world of high pressure living and alcoholism. 07–0078 $2.95.

LET ME BE A WOMAN. Best selling author Elisabeth Elliot (author of *THROUGH GATES OF SPLENDOR*) presents her profound and unique perspective on womanhood. This is a significant book on a continuing controversial subject. 07–2162 $2.95.

WE'RE IN THE ARMY NOW by Imeldia Morris Eller. Five children become their older brother's "army" as they work together to keep their family intact during a time of crisis for their mother. 07–7862 $2.95.

WILD CHILD by Mari Hanes. A heartrending story of a young boy who was abandoned and struggled alone for survival. You will be moved as you read how one woman's love tames this boy who was more animal than human. 07–8224 $2.95.

THE SURGEON'S FAMILY by David Hernandez with Carole Gift Page. This is an incredible three-generation story of a family that has faced danger and death — and has survived. Walking dead-end streets of violence and poverty, often seemingly without hope, the family of David Hernandez has struggled to find a new kind of life. 07–6684 $2.95.

The books listed are available at your bookstore. If unavailable, send check with order to cover retail price plus 10% for postage and handling to:

Tyndale House Publishers, Inc.
Box 80
Wheaton, Illinois 60189

Prices and availability subject to change without notice. Allow 4–6 weeks for delivery.